Reviews

This little book is a big reminder for us to be ever so mindful of our direction of travel in life. Thank you for sharing your experiences, and your encouragement to change our direction as needed so we can all finally experience the *Joy Beyond the Road*.
—Linda Steinbacher, Good Friend

Joy is the operative word for this book's theme. The joy and peace of friends and family stories that God's presence has touched is prominent. As you read it, the love of God and demonstrated to God, is indeed inspiring and up lifting. Your heart will be touched.
—Sharon Foster, Friend and Paralegal

The author has a God given gift of prose and poetry. Here the reader has an opportunity to see God's love for us, the hope of our salvation and experience the blessings of today. Journey with her through this small book and discover God's love reflected through kindness to each other. You will find a new understanding of many Bible verses and learn how to "Practice His Presence" in your life. *Joy Beyond the Road* can be read many times to find new nuggets of truth, or to re-center yourself in the love of Christ. It is a beautiful read and should be kept on your nightstand for your daily devotions.
—Mary Ann Rule, Controller, Energenics Corp.; Board Chair, Naples Adventist Christian School

I have enjoyed reading her stories and seeing how God has blessed her in the past. One can see how, as a result of these experiences, she has been able to share with those who may be treading where she has been.
—Art Preuss Pastor, Naples Seventh-day Adventist Church

Joy Beyond the Road

Marlene Smith

TEACH Services, Inc.
PUBLISHING
www.TEACHServices.com • (800) 367-1844

Copyright © 2022 Marlene Smith
Copyright © 2022 TEACH Services, Inc.
ISBN-13: 978-1-4796-1463-9 (Paperback)
ISBN-13: 978-1-4796-1464-6 (ePub)

Published by

TEACH Services, Inc.
PUBLISHING
www.TEACHServices.com • (800) 367-1844

Table of Contents

Chapter 1

I just finished the book *Pilgrim's Progress* by John Bunyan, and in the closing chapters, I felt so drawn to Jesus that I just wanted to see Him face-to-face. During the writing of these pages, the coronavirus is spreading worldwide, and fear and trembling are apparent. While others may be in that category, I am not. With confidence and peace, I enter this new era from which there is only one way to escape.

I'm sure you have seen pictures of people wearing and waving a large foam hand with the index finger pointing upward. Yes, this shows that Jesus is the way, the truth, and the life. Perhaps that finger is pointing to tangible things so present in our society—that beautiful car (and the insurance company); the beautiful home (with just the color siding you want); the piece of art that would go lovely in your living room (for the exorbitant price—plus you just should insure it!).

So, for you, where is the finger pointing? Horizontally or vertically? If you are honest with yourself, you probably want it both ways (a little bit of heaven with a little bit of treasure on earth). Now, don't get me wrong. There is nothing intrinsically wrong with having a nice car or home or art in that home. But does your pride in "things" exceed your desire for a heavenly home? How weighty is your scale? Which side is the heaviest? Don't answer, or your honesty might surprise you.

> *Now, naturally, most of us don't lead charmed lives where nothing goes awry. In those cases, we still can give thanks to God that He is there with us (Ps. 16:10-11). As a matter of fact, read the whole Psalm and be uplifted!*

There are times in life that God is speaking to you—even when you are not aware of His voice. But I tell you that He is doing His best to get your attention. Many times, it seems like you're doing everything right. All good things are falling into place, and you thank yourself for your "smarts." Man! Don't you think for a moment that it's you! For "[e]very good gift and every perfect gift is from above, and comes down from the Father" (James 1:17). So, give thanks to Him as you walk the road in this life to the next. Now, naturally, most of us don't lead charmed lives where nothing goes awry. In those cases, we still can give thanks to God that He is there with us (Ps. 16:10-11). As a matter of fact, read the whole Psalm and be uplifted! In many lives in this sinful world, nothing goes right. There is so much—too much—sickness, death, tears, to the point of hopelessness, like, "What's the use of even trying?" We are so attuned to our emotions that the fact of life hereafter and forever doesn't give us the hope we should have. So, what's the remedy? The vertical finger points the way. He says He will never leave us nor forsake us (Heb. 13:5). What courage that should give us! To know that He is always with us, and/or sends angels to guard us on our way, is a tremendous joy to our hearts. It's truly the "peace that passes understanding."

Speaking of walking in the right way reminds me of the time years ago that I had an appointment with a car insurance company that was in the next town from my home. I didn't know exactly where it was but felt confident that I would find it. There was no GPS in those days. I came upon the road so suddenly and so quickly that I turned right—right into the parking lot. I did the business at hand and was in the car thinking, "OK, I turned right into the parking lot, so I have to turn left to get on the way back. Much to my dismay, I was going the wrong way on a one-way road—a main road at that! What to do? Pray! God immediately answered. There were no cars coming and only a couple of cars passed by at the U-turn where I just blended into the correct stream of traffic. No one can tell me that it was just a coincidence that traffic was light in both directions. No! It was God through angels who orchestrated that divine emergency. I could see on the face of the driver behind whom I was going to emerge that he was beyond surprised—maybe shocked—that I was coming out of that one-way street almost parallel with him! But no accident. It went just fine and like they say, "smooth move." ☺ That's my Friend for you. Always there, even when you're wrong. But you must ask for His presence, invite Him into your struggles, and He's right there to help you. So, as soon as you ask, thank Him also. He just loves you so much, and to hear you call on Him warms His heart of love.

Chapter 2

L ooking down the road to the future, everyone has hope for something better. There's always that stretch of the imagination that we want to believe that further on is that "something better." And, for everyone, there is.

In this time of coronavirus, there are numerous ways to keep from boredom in the house (because of self-quarantining) and several ways to stay clean and healthy. Most of them are common sense and ways we've lived in the fifties through the eighties and nineties. Clean hands and a pure heart (Ps. 24:4-5), water (Isa. 44:3), and bread and water (Exod. 23:25). Don't mope because "[a] merry heart doeth good like a medicine" (Prov. 17:22, KJV) or "cheerful countenance" as Proverbs 15:13 (KJV) says.

On our road, we will discover points of interest. One year, while living in the northeast, autumn was in full display of glorious colors right on the road to my home. The multicolored trees lined the road and the tippy tops bent over to meet their neighbor's tree across the road, creating a beautiful tunnel-like landscape. So, my husband and I decided to take a day trip to view other similar areas and autumn's beautiful presentations. Our home in Massachusetts was about a mile from the border of New Hampshire, so we headed in that direction. I am empty of the best words of how to describe the beauty as we traveled to the Vermont border from New Hampshire. Nevertheless, I was full to overflowing with praise and thanks to God for allowing this once-in-a-lifetime *ooooh* and *ahhhh* trip! There is beauty on the way to the end of the road.

Other points of interest on the way to the end of the road are those lovely people I've encountered. There are so very many, but I'll name a few (not their real names). I'm reminded of bustling Betty who was a director of Sabbath School for many years. Everyone who did their job—well or not so well—got

a rush of compliments from Betty. You were so thankful and appreciative of it that you just wanted to do your very best for her. She just showed loving-kindness to everyone. Never a frown on her face.

In our small church, there was booming Brad, whose directing of song service was a challenge to say the least. Oh, he had a strong vibrant voice all right, but one time it was too much to take, and the worshippers were trying to stifle their laughter! What had started out with the pianist playing a few notes of introduction so that we would be ready to sing, became another song as Brad belted out a familiar hymn but not the one we were to sing. He got a little ahead of himself before he realized the pianist was playing something so different from what he was singing, and no one else was singing, so he just stopped, looked at the pianist with a frown, and said, "You're playing the wrong song!" Then, embarrassed, he said, "I guess I was singing the wrong song—sorry." On with song service. 😊

On the way to the end of the road, I could always count on friendly Frances for direction, for help, for beauty in the way she would arrange things. I think I learned a lot of ways to present things that would copy her expertise in presentation. That could include baking, cooking, dining experiences, and flower arrangements—just to name a few. Her love of beauty was even in the way she talked about God and especially what He plans for us. I dreamily think about her when I read the last two chapters of Revelation (21 and 22).

Chapter 3

O n the road, there will always be signs for you to follow so that you'll know if you're on the right one, headed toward the ultimate end of your journey. But perhaps you missed a sign somewhere because the majority of the traffic is going left, and you sensed you should be turning to the Right Way. But you dismiss that thought and keep bearing left. Pretty soon, there's a bump in the road. But it's only a slight one—like that "little lie" that you thought didn't matter. And then you remembered that you had to cover that lie with another falsehood that ruined a friendship. But that's in the past, so forget it. Oops! A bigger bump and a rut. Now this is getting serious. And the thoughts start tumbling out of your mind of all the many ruts that have taken you this far, so you want no more of this road! Therefore, STOP, reverse direction—who knows how much worse it could become— get back as quickly as possible to where the road bore the slight turn to the left. So, you leave it and turn to the Right road that

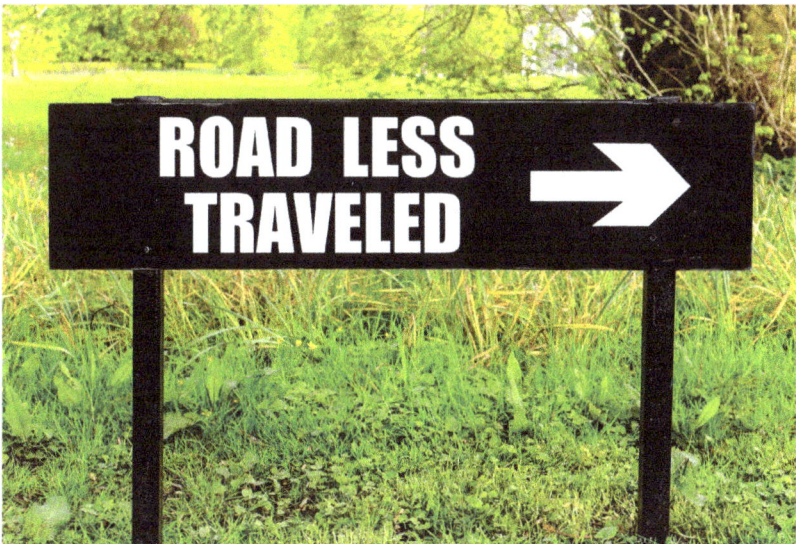

was traveled less. Sure enough, signs pointing to the Way ahead are clearly marked.

It's time to fill up the vehicle you're in so there won't be any more delays. While there at the Stop, you meet my friend, helpful Harry. What a nice guy. As soon as he closes up shop, he'll be going the same way you are. I met Harry quite a few years ago. He and his wife, smiling Sue, were giving words of blessing as I entered the church. Harry is the kind of guy looking for ways to make one comfortable and cared about. If you needed a repair on anything, he'd find someone to help you if he himself couldn't fix it. Every conversation with him would almost be a Bible study as he inter-jected Scripture along with a practical application. Sometimes I would chuckle at the way he would analyze a situation to meet the equal of a Bible verse he just quoted. But, to me, it made sense. ☺ His wife would give a wink and a smile and a nod of her head to agree. Great people I'll meet at journey's end.

Back on the road, we've gone a little way, but wait! It looks like … it is! Ron and Rhonda. I haven't seen them in years! And here they are, just walking leisurely down the road. I must stop and talk to them. Together, they shouted out, "Hey, look who it is!" We hugged and I was so glad to see this cute couple. Rhonda is very talented as her fingers glide over the keyboard, and Ron is smiling broadly as he is so proud of her. As we traveled the road together, Ron started a conversation with, "What do you make of the world as it is today? Are you afraid of the situations financially, politically, socially?" As we traveled on, he bowed his head and I thought he was going to pray. But no, he was just collecting his thoughts in order to say it right: "I truly believe this is the right road to the very end of time. So much is going on around us, but I have a sense of peace, the sense of being led, and a sense of being cared for. It must be the presence of the Holy Spirit."

I was glad to hear him say that because that's how I was feeling too. Rhonda then added, "I'm so glad we're traveling this road together. It's so good to talk about how each of us have had our trials and, through prayer and helping each other, we have come this far on this beautiful road."

Then, to lighten the conversation, Ron added, "Yes, we may have been cold, but thank God we weren't frozen!" "Chosen," I corrected. "And "called" we were. That's why we're on this less traveled road." You know, don't you, that having loving company along life's way is so comforting. You can just relax and be your-self—knowing He's got your back.

Chapter 4

Howerver, just because you're on the right road, straight and narrow as it is and full of blessings, the devil won't stop annoying you. Whenever something good happens, he has to try to turn it into a negative situation to try to pull you away from the "It is written." So, let's go there … to His Word. Turn to Exodus 20 as we begin this part of the journey that we're already on.

1. God is reminding us of who He is, the Lord our God who loves and blesses us and will keep us close to Him, if we so desire (Exod. 20:1-2). After all, look at what He has

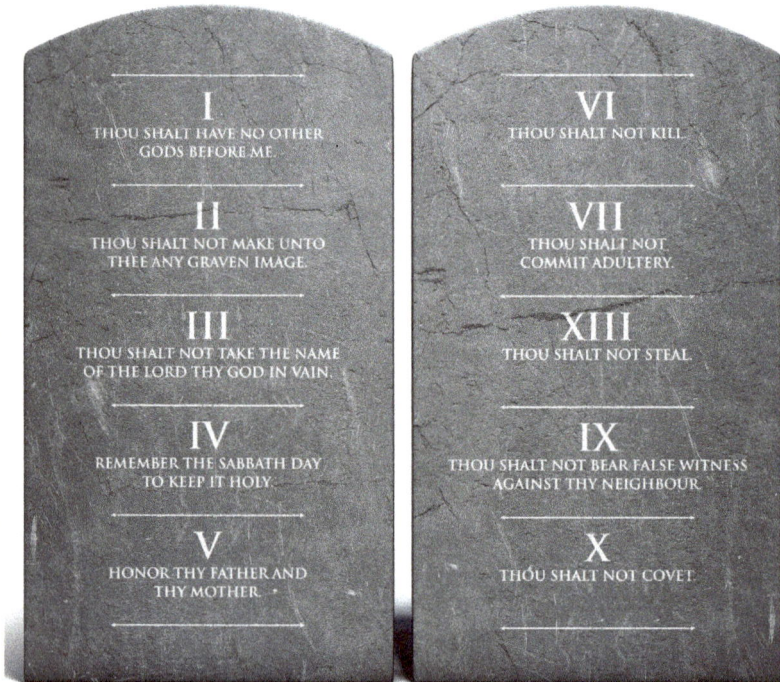

I THOU SHALT HAVE NO OTHER GODS BEFORE ME.	VI THOU SHALT NOT KILL.
II THOU SHALT NOT MAKE UNTO THEE ANY GRAVEN IMAGE.	VII THOU SHALT NOT COMMIT ADULTERY.
III THOU SHALT NOT TAKE THE NAME OF THE LORD THY GOD IN VAIN.	XIII THOU SHALT NOT STEAL.
IV REMEMBER THE SABBATH DAY TO KEEP IT HOLY.	IX THOU SHALT NOT BEAR FALSE WITNESS AGAINST THY NEIGHBOUR.
V HONOR THY FATHER AND THY MOTHER.	X THOU SHALT NOT COVET.

already done in your life. He always gives us roses when He has squelched the thorns. There's no one in this whole world that can possibly say that their whole life was negative. He knew you before you were born (Isa. 44:2) and loved you through your mistakes. Even so much that He died for you (John 3:16) so He could take you to be with Him when He returns (John 14:1-3). That time is not too far distant.

2. I love God so much that I don't worship any other gods (Exod. 3-6). There are some people who worship the many gods of this transient world. We can worship self by hoarding all kinds of things that we "want" but really don't "need." We can worship something so worthless as to ignore the needs of others. Have you seen yourself in that mirror? We look askance at those people generations ago who made statues of gold and silver and bowed down to them and, yes, even prayed to them for "good luck." This kind of worship is only hurting the generations that follow if not "nipped in the bud." Yet, God shows mercy to the millions who love Him and keep His commandments.

3. Have you met anyone whose speech always includes God's name? I don't mean in prayer. No, I mean in vain! (Verse 7.) It hurts my ears, and I'm offended. I wonder how God feels! When I have had the opportunity to squeeze in during the conversation, I ask, "Oh, are you calling on my God for something? He hears you, you know."

4. As we continue to worship the true God, we can be close to Him every day. But God has set aside a particular day to leave your worries and anxieties with Him (verses 8-11). In Genesis 2:3, He has made holy and sanctified the seventh day of the week for you to be closer to Him and to recognize Him as your Creator. It's a day of resting in His love, His overpowering love, that He showed at the cross. When we PHP (Practice His Presence), a calm overrules our whole being. It's such a peaceful existence basking in the Sonshine of His love. While Practicing His Presence, we are aware of His closeness as He gives thoughts and holy

ideas as to how to worship Him on this day. He wants His Holy Spirit to infuse you with His kind of love for others that by serving others, you are doing it to Him. God made the seventh-day Sabbath for all of mankind. He has no favorites. We all, each and every one of us, are His favorite. I love my God of the Sabbath. On this seventh day of the week, Saturday, I have often felt an aura, an intangible thing around me. It's nothing that I can adequately explain, so I'll just say that it must be the presence of the Holy Spirit! I just bask in it! Someday soon we will all have that experience when worshipping Him in His holy temple of the New Jerusalem.

5. Nowadays, there are so many dysfunctional families, and God is sad about that. If only at the beginning of life we all had shown respect and love to our parents, maybe it would be a different world today. Following God's command to honor our parents can come about when we first love God (Exod. 20:12). After all, He first loved us. Dysfunction shows up in various ways. It can start with just the faintest idea that we are in control of all things within our realm of existence. You know, the "my way or the highway" mentality. Instead of acquiescing to a favor, we tend to think, "What's in it for me?" Friends, that's not a godly way. Respectfully answering a favor or questions should be forthcoming if we say we love God. OK, so what would Jesus say or do? You'd know if you were Practicing His Presence. Further down the road, when children are no longer children, it'll all come back to you. Like, why didn't I say or do such and so? Of course, you can't go back and undo the bad things. But Jesus can make all things good and possible again when we seek His forgiveness. Just ask and you'll see the changes in yourself and in your family.

6. When one starts a hateful thought of someone, Satan is there to advance the ideas of carrying out malicious actions. Don't go there. Don't commit murder to get even (verse 13)! Don't even let lingering thoughts overtake you. Sometimes we can kill with words. But unless those words

are tempered by the Holy Spirit, "which is in you" (1 Cor. 6:19), nothing good can come out of it. Remember that God loves those whom we don't love. So, pray for the love of Christ to return to your heart and don't kill or murder or hate that one who Christ died for, just as He died for you.

7. If you are cautious of your words and maintain Practicing His Presence, you won't fall into the temptation of adulterous thoughts or the actions that sometimes, unfortunately, follow (Exod. 20:14). Keep your minds on the best things about your spouse. There are numerous reasons that you married her/him, so review those reasons and say them to your spouse aloud and often. Keep your mind on the happiest days of your life, review them with each other. Laugh a lot! Smile at your spouse in times she/he would not be expecting it. Tell your children, older or younger, how much you love their mother/father. Praying together is the surest way to keep any other person from being involved in your relationship. The only third party in a marriage is Jesus Christ Himself, who loves both of you.

8. Taking what you want from someone else is stealing (verse 15). There are several ways to steal. We consider the thief who breaks into our home and takes precious possessions, worthy of jail time. Of course, prison is also the place for those who steal credit cards and personal IDs, popularly known as identify theft. But have you ever considered another form of stealing? I'm talking about taking someone else's words of importance and then claiming them as your own. The reason for this is so that you will feel important, and pride overrules. Now your enemy has found a home in your mind. Another way to steal is to take away the joy and happiness from a friend who got a promotion by downplaying it and thinking you deserved it more. Therefore, no compliment. You are withholding (stealing?) appreciation for a person so blessed by God that it ruins a friendship! Don't be like that. Enter into a mindset of praise and thanksgiving for what you have

and for where you are in life. But the worst step yet is to steal from God. He has given you so many blessings, so why haven't you acknowledged that by giving back what is already His (Mal. 3)? Why do you withhold your tithe, first and foremost, and offerings of your thankfulness? Well, thankfully, you do give. Therefore, you have peace and comfort from His grace.

9. Lying lips are an abomination to the Lord (Prov. 6:16-9; 12:22; Exod. 20:16). "'Oh what a tangled web we weave, when first we practice to deceive,'"[1] How bad can lying get? Well, just look at destroyed marriages, political downfalls, personal angst, and all the other forms that lead even to murder. The worst is that you wonder if you can trust anyone again—even family members! There is Someone you can trust. His name is Jesus. Or maybe you hoped He was lying when He said "[B]e sure your sin will find you out" (Num. 32:23), or "[T]he wages of sin *is* death" (Rom. 6:23). No, no, we believe that Jesus' death on the cross was FOR us, the forgiveness of sin for all the liars who ask for forgiveness. There is hope for all in the cross of Christ.

10. The thought of coveting is sometimes not thought of as sinful. You might "like" your neighbor's car better than your own or his/her house or "anything that *is* your neighbor's" (Exod. 20:17). As long as it doesn't border on jealousy or envy, you may be OK. But be sure your heart and mind are in agreement that you don't want to sin; so then, turn your thoughts away from this and get back on the road to joy. Besides, you're content with what God has blessed you with, right?

[1] Walter Scott, Brainy Quotes, https://1ref.us/1s9 (accessed November 8, 2021).

Chapter 5

I've only touched lightly on the Ten Commandments because I want to get us back on the road to safety, the road that leads to complete joy. When we have the commandments inside of us, as the Holy Spirit is, there's no thought of sinning. Our minds are only on good and helpful ways to live. That's not to say that there won't be glitches along the road, but know that God is with you and will never forsake you (Heb. 13:5). What a comforting promise. Think seriously what that means: never forsake you. The Creator of the universe! God—in Jesus and through the Holy Spirit—stands beside you every moment of every day! How cool is that?! Feeling safer now? Feeling more at ease and peace? You should—if you are Practicing His Presence.

Day after day, I Practice His Presence out of pure love for Him and the security I sense by it. Not a day passes that I'm not aware of His love for me. Through His Holy Spirit's direction and guidance, He is my all in all. Did you know that His plan was made for you before you were even born? Yes, He tells us so in Isaiah 44:2 and reminds us in Psalm 139:14 that you were "fearfully *and* wonderfully made." How much He loves you!

I wish that when the coronavirus passes, we won't go back to normal. We need the new normal of being kinder and more thoughtful and more helpful than was the old normal. Right now, I don't see that happening. As a matter of fact, the newspapers are full of more kinds of greed than I have ever experienced! This comes under the laws of lying and stealing, not loving God or your neighbor. I believe that greed is the motivating power that will lead to one's final destruction.

Yet, there's hope for all—everyone—because we all are sinners … and we have that hope in the broken body of Christ, our Savior, who nailed all our sins with Him on the cruel cross. 1 John 1:9 says, "If we confess our sins, He is faithful and just to forgive us *our* sins and to cleanse us from all unrighteousness." Yes, that's

"*Did you know that His plan was made for you before you were even born? Yes, He tells us so in Isaiah 44:2 and reminds us in Psalm 139:14 that you were "fearfully and wonderfully made." How much He loves you!*

a big IF. We can say we're sorry, but that's a bit short of asking forgiveness for the sin that so often returns with a vengeance. When you ask for forgiveness, God knows your penitent heart and forgives you instantly and blesses you with a new start.

So, as we continue on the road, our hearts are warmed by the fact that Jesus is on the road with us and has given us strength to abide whatever is ahead. The "whatever" will be for the good of our growth in grace, unpleasant though it may be. We don't know why certain things happen in our lives to interrupt our mundane or listless occupation of time here on earth. But whatever it is, God knows and directs and guides us on our way to the end of the road. He wants us to know Him, to love and trust Him in all things, tangent and invisible, because He loves us and cares for us (1 Peter 5:7).

Chapter 6

When my oldest son was seven years old, it would be his first experience away from home. The church's junior camp was coming up and he wanted to go. So, arrangements were made to take him and his friend to the campground in the next state with his friend's parents driving. I made up his little suitcase with the clothes for the week along with extra provisions for the ride or when he got to camp. The week went by pretty quickly as care for his three younger brothers entailed the busyness that calls for daily baths, washing clothes and hanging them out on the clothesline, and, of course, changing diapers. So, it was with joy and anticipation that I looked forward to the return of camper son that following Sunday. Here he came in smiling and happy to be home too. Full of the things he wanted to tell me about camp, he flung his suitcase to the floor, and I received a big hug. One thing I noticed was that he was wearing the same outfit that I sent him in the previous Sunday. Oh, well, he must have worn all the clothes in the suitcase and returned to the outfit he'd been sent away in. So, I better get the dirty clothes out of the suitcase and into the washing machine. Opening it up and seeing, not dirty clothes, but all the clean clothes I packed for him still folded exactly how I had put them in! This child had not used the clothing provided for him for a full week! Why not? A shrug of his shoulders was his non-caring answer. So why am I telling you this story so many years later? For one thing, he's no longer embarrassed by it and secondly it brings out the point that even though I had provided the necessities, he didn't take advantage of them. He chose to just stay as he was when he left.

How is it with you, friend? Have you accepted the Master Tailor's robe that He designed and provided for you? Or are you just as comfortable as you were last year? Only you can answer those questions. But it behooves you to take stock now as time is short and shorter for some more than for others. We never know when our last day will be. God, through Jesus and the Holy Spirit, has provided all—everything you need for your salvation.

So then, this road we're on should be free from trouble, right? No, you can't say that. BUT, with it, there is Someone who is right beside you, going with you through the high waters of life so you won't be overcome. Don't forget—HE is the Master of the waters, and HE will see you through the highest wave of oppression and give you peace for your soul.

I would now like to turn your attention to the end of the road and beyond. Just at the very end of this world, as we know it, will come several earth-shattering pestilences that will affect everyone in some way, be it through family experience or knowledge of its happenings through word of mouth or media. Right now, in 2020, we are experiencing COVID-19 in the whole world. Not that everyone has it, but that every cognizant person is aware of it. There is no antidote or cure for it. Thankfully, all people in the medical sciences are working feverishly to find the answer. So, what happens after the coronavirus pandemic is reduced to epidemic class and then to a less frightening "bug" going around? Certainly, a new "normal" will be entered into out of necessity. Perhaps thoughts

of God and Jesus will be more warmly received—and that is as it should be for your peace of mind.

Philippians 2:5 says to have the mind of Christ, thus Practicing His Presence and having the Holy Spirit within us will guide us through everyday choices of activities. When we do Practice His Presence, it will be evident to those we meet each day. Who knows what influence you might be to lead someone to the cross of Christ and acccpt His love. Even at the end of the road, it's OK "If we confess our sins, He is faithful and just to forgive us *our* sins and to cleanse us from ALL unrighteousness" (1 John 1:9, emphasis mine). What a fantastic promise that is! It is then that we face the future unafraid and with peace that passes understanding.

The joy just beyond the end of the road must be that heaven has its doors open wide to you. No longer the narrow way with all its foible, cares, and frustrations but the wonderful life eternal that Jesus has come to take us to when He comes the second time. He's reaching down His hand to lift you up from drowning in this world of sin.

> " *The joy just beyond the end of the road must be that heaven has its doors open wide to you.*

Chapter 7

Years ago, Dan and I were doing some day traveling. This one day we took a winding road that went along Swift River in New Hampshire. Truly, the water is swift as it travels over, under, and around rocks. Some places you could jump from rounded rock to a flat rock if you had the agility to do so. Dan and I did and had fun doing it. Along the way, were pretty little waterfalls with rushing waters. As we were on a flat rock watching the waters and taking in all the beauty, we noticed a little boy trying to traverse the rocks, when suddenly he slipped into the waters that were going swiftly at the waterfall. Somehow, he got flipped over on the edge of the falls and grabbed on to a rock, holding on for dear life. But he could not pull himself up over the falls. All he could do was hold on to the rock with the most pitiful look of fright on his face. When Dan realized the boy was in deep trouble, he immediately went to him, balanced on a rock on top of the falls, and extended his hand to the boy. The boy realized he would have to let go with one hand to allow Dan to pull him up out of the dangerous place he was in. The boy bravely let go with one hand, reaching up to Dan. Without hesitation, Dan quickly grabbed his hand and pulled him up and out of the dangerous waters. Dan made sure the boy was safe and on his way out of Swift River and on his way back to his mother. Dan came back to me on the flat rock, and we both looked at that sweet reunion of mother and son. That mother was close enough to us, and on the grassy area by the edge, she knew we could hear her say, "Thank you so much. Thank you for saving my son's life. Yes, you saved his life."

In like manner, Jesus reaches down His nail-pierced hand with loving eyes and is longing to save you from being overcome by the enticing waters of this world. Reach back up to Him and He will save you—save you for eternity!

The sheer joy and happiness you will find is easily understood as you read Revelation 21 revealing God's gift of a "new heaven and a new earth, for the first heaven and the first earth had passed away" (verse 1). "And God will wipe away every tear from their eyes … no more death, nor sorrow, nor crying …. no more pain … former things have passed away" (verse 4). What more could one ask for? But there is much, much more. From the description of the New Jerusalem in glorious colors and size to the best of all—seeing Jesus face to face! Continuing in Revelation 22 is God's love in giving us all that we could ask for and more. No matter what version of the Bible you read, your heart will have a special peace and yearn for that time when you finally have the Joy Beyond the Road. Today is your beginning—accept His hand.

Oh! To see You face to face,

To know the depth of saving grace!

I'll hug You tightly

And You'll smile brightly

As we enter that Heavenly place!

TEACH Services, Inc.
P U B L I S H I N G

We invite you to view the complete
selection of titles we publish at:
www.TEACHServices.com

We encourage you to write us
with your thoughts about this,
or any other book we publish at:
info@TEACHServices.com

TEACH Services' titles may be purchased in
bulk quantities for educational, fund-raising,
business, or promotional use.
bulksales@TEACHServices.com

Finally, if you are interested in seeing
your own book in print, please contact us at:
publishing@TEACHServices.com
We are happy to review your manuscript at no charge.